Divorce : A New Adventure

Marriage Break Up Secrets

Heather E. Shores

Table of Contents

Chapter Ten

Conclusion: Embracing the Journey

Ahead

Introduction

In this journey called life, we often encounter unexpected twists and turns, moments that change the course of our existence. For me, that pivotal moment came in the form of a divorce—a profound and life-altering experience that propelled me into uncharted territory. As I sit here, penning these words, I can't help but feel a deep sense of connection to you, the reader who now holds this book in your hands. I know what you're going through. I've been there.

Divorce. The very word carries weight, laden with a mix of emotions—heartache, confusion, anger, and fear. It's a word that often leaves us feeling lost, grappling with the unknown. However, through my own personal journey and the experiences of those closest to me, I have come to realize that divorce is not something to be faced blindly, without adequate preparation or guidance.

In my circle of friends, an intimate group of men and women, four out of six of us, including myself, have walked the path of divorce. We have seen the shattered dreams, the painful unraveling of once-vowed forever love, and the complexities that arise when a union dissolves.

Each story is unique, with its own set of challenges and triumphs, but we all share a common thread—a profound understanding of the emotions and uncertainties that accompany divorce.

It is with this shared understanding and empathy that I have penned "Divorce: A New Adventure - Marriage Breakup Secrets." This book is not just a collection of words on paper; it is a lifeline, a beacon of light to guide you through the stormy seas of divorce. I invite you to embark on this journey with me, to delve into the depths of your emotions and emerge stronger, wiser, and ready to embrace the new adventure that awaits.

Within the pages of this book, you will find a treasure trove of insights, knowledge, and practical advice gained through personal experience and the wisdom of others who have walked this path before us. We will navigate the complexities of divorce, acknowledging that no two stories are the same, while empowering you to rise above the challenges and come out as your best self.

We will navigate the complex terrain of legal proceedings, ensuring that you are armed with the information you need to protect your rights and make informed decisions.

But it doesn't stop there. Divorce becomes even more intricate when children are involved, as was the case in my own journey.

We will discuss the delicate balance of co-parenting, offering strategies to prioritize the well-being of your children while navigating the sometimes turbulent waters of post-divorce relationships.

This literary piece goes beyond being a mere manual; it emerges as a true ally and partner. It's a heartfelt conversation with someone who has walked the path, stumbled, and found her way again. Together, we will explore the emotional healing process, learning to forgive ourselves and others, and embracing the opportunity for personal growth and transformation.

Now, I can't promise that this journey will be easy. There will be moments when you feel overwhelmed, when the weight of it all threatens to pull you under. However, during such instances, always bear in mind that you are not isolated. You have a community of fellow travelers, myself included, who are here to offer support, encouragement, and understanding.

So, breathe in deeply and flip the page. Let the words within these chapters ignite a fire within you, sparking a newfound resilience and determination. The adventure awaits, and you are ready. Let's embark on this journey together and discover the secrets that will empower you to reclaim your life after divorce.

Chapter One

Embracing Change and Growth

Unpredictable and surprising events are woven into the tapestry of life. You are holding this book at the beginning of a new chapter in your life, one that will be distinguished by the difficulties of divorce. It's a sad chapter about goodbyes and broken hearts, but it also shows how strong the human spirit can be. It's an open invitation to explore new territory, learn to swim in the unfamiliar waters of transformation, and find the inner resources for self-improvement.

Dear reader, a divorce is not a simple process. It's an emotional landscape as turbulent as the open ocean. Your dreams are destroyed as waves of anguish wash up on the shores of your soul. Here, among the rubble of the old world, is where you find yourself now. You are, however, not alone; this much we can promise.

This book is our way of reaching out to you and offering support while you navigate the unfamiliar waters of divorce. We intend to be a source of comfort, direction, and insight for you. We can relate to the fear in your heart and the doubt in your intellect. But the possibility to start over, to reimagine one's life, and to recover from the depths of sorrow with newfound strength is a germinating seed within this ambiguity.

Acceptance is the first step towards embracing change. The ability to accept that one's life has taken an unexpected turn but still have the fortitude to do so. Realizing that endings can pave the way for new beginnings and that development can occur even in the most challenging of circumstances. The sweet and sour tune of change invites you to move to the beat of your own fortitude.

It's crucial to be kind to yourself as you set out on this new journey. Tears heal the heart's wounds, so let them flow freely. Be with those who love and support you through this difficult time; their presence will be a rock of stability. Seek solace in the arms of experts who can help you navigate the legal and emotional hurdles of divorce.

Healing is not a straight line, so please keep that in mind. It's as unique to you as your fingerprint, and it happens in its own sweet time. Allow yourself to experience all of your feelings, for they are the paint with which you will decorate your new world.

Recognize that it is in the cracks and crevices where genuine development can take place.

In the following pages, we'll discuss how to handle the many complex feelings that come along with co-parenting, as well as the financial adjustments that are often necessary. We'll talk about ways to take care of oneself, how to mend broken relationships, and how to plan for the future. We shall go forth together into the exciting new world that awaits us.

As you begin this new chapter, dear reader, take comfort in the knowledge that you have the fortitude within to endure any difficulty that may come your way. Your strength of character, rather than your luck of birth, will determine your ultimate destiny. Use this book as a map to lead you to a more promising future, one where you can experience profound personal growth and ultimately come into full contact with the authentic, wise version of yourself.

Dear Reader, we hope you enjoy the ride. I pray that you will be changed forever by this experience and that you will learn about yourself and find the strength to persevere in the face of adversity.

Chapter Two

Navigating Emotional Challenges: Grief and Healing

Emotions are like wild vines in the maze of divorce; they wrap themselves around everything. Inquiring Minds, Here I am, a fellow survivor, someone who has been where you are and come out the other side. As we begin this new chapter together, I want to assure you of my support, compassion, and assurance that you may find peace once again.

Grief is an unwanted companion when a marriage has ended. It makes its home in the crevices of your soul, throwing shadows across familiar terrain. It gently nudges you toward regret by suggesting that you revisit the past. You may take comfort in the idea that your suffering is recognized, comprehended, and shared at these times of loss.

Dear reader, it is important that you give yourself permission to grieve. Feel free to cry all your whispered words and unrealized hopes away. Sob for the lost romance and broken promises that have cluttered your way. You'll discover the fortitude to recover and move on in this exposed place, for resilience is conceived in the arms of loss.

Recognize that recovery is not a straight line. The route twists and turns in ways you wouldn't imagine. On those days when it seems like everything is piled on top of you, every little thing you try to accomplish seems like a Herculean endeavor. On others, however, you may feel a glimmer of optimism and discover oases of joy among the ruins.

Be encouraged by the efficacy of self-care, reader. Take care of your mental, physical, and spiritual selves as though they were delicate flowers.

Find relief in things that calm and soothe you, like taking a stroll in the park, reading a book you love, or listening to music that speaks to your heart. Find a way to express yourself creatively, in writing, or by talking to someone you trust who won't judge you.

It is essential to keep in mind, during emotional turmoil, that you are not alone. Get help from people who care about you, such as friends, family, or a therapist. They can listen to your struggles and help you figure out how to go forward. Put yourself in the company of positive people who will help you remember your own power and value. Give their company a chance to heal your broken heart.

Please be patient with the healing process, dear reader. Like a flower slowly pushing through the soil, this unfolding is soft and gradual. Remember that there is no time limit on grieving. Indulge in the lulls, the flashes of hope, for they are pointing the way to a future filled with opportunity.

Keep in mind that your feelings are normal and your path is special as we move through this new chapter together. Rather than being defined by the anguish of your divorce, your strength of character will. Grief can open up previously undiscovered depths and strengths within a person if they let it.

As we move forward, dear reader, please keep in mind that restoration is possible. Even if the road ahead is rocky and the feelings are intense, know that you are not alone. Let us weather the waves of sorrow together and emerge on the other side more resilient and compassionate.

Chapter Three

Building a Support System: Finding Strength in Relationships

There is an undeniable void in financial stability after a divorce. Having set out on this perilous path myself, I know the comfort and fortitude that can be found in the arms of one's loved ones. I applaud you for seeing the value of reaching out for help if you are holding this book in your hands.

It is not a show of weakness to admit you need help; rather, it is a recognition of our common humanity and our innate need for community. You are ready to make connections that will raise you and carry you through the difficulties ahead since you are reading these words.

Recognizing that you need help from others to get through this is the first step towards assembling that help. Seek support from those who have already proven to be reliable, whether they be members of your family, close friends, or a professional counselor. Tell them about yourself — your hopes, your worries, and your narrative. Don't be afraid to put yourself out there and let people see the real you.

Recognize the importance of belonging to a group. Seek out counseling or support organizations that cater to those going through a divorce. In these groups, people can feel comfortable opening up about their lives and receiving support from others who truly understand. You can discover acceptance, direction, and the knowledge that you are not alone by associating with people who have been where you are.

Carefully select your circle of confidants; not all friendships are equal. Put yourself in the company of people who will encourage you, who will listen to you without passing judgment, and who will always have your back. You can take comfort in their company, in their capacity to reassure you of your value even when you doubt it. Lean on them because they are the bedrock your heart can rest on.

Developing a network of people who have your back requires not just taking, but also giving. Treat these connections with the respect and appreciation they deserve. It's important to be there for other people, even if you're feeling overwhelmed. Give them your undivided attention, reassuring words, and a shoulder to cry on. The ties that form as a result of shared experiences are formed in the fires of empathy and kindness.

Keep in mind that you don't have to go through a divorce alone. It's a tapestry stitched together with the strands of solidarity and perseverance. When you surround yourself with caring people, you give yourself the power of shared experiences and the comfort of human connection. When you're around people who truly get you, you'll feel a surge of positivity and be reminded that you're never truly alone.

Let us celebrate the strength of our connections as we move through this new chapter of our lives together. Don't be afraid to reach out for help if you need it; it's through our mutual exposure to weakness that we learn and grow the most. Allow other people to love, guide, and strengthen you, and be willing to do the same. Let us create a fabric of strength, kindness, and unending encouragement.

You may turn your healing and growth journey after divorce into an extraordinary adventure if you embrace the beauty of constructing a support system. If you extend a hand, many others will be there to take it and lend you their unflinching support. You are not alone on this journey; we are bound together by our common experiences and the support we provide and receive from one another.

Chapter Four

Legal Considerations: Understanding the Divorce Process

Divorce is a difficult journey that involves more than just emotional fortitude; it also necessitates an in-depth understanding of the legal complexities at play. Having been through a divorce myself, I can relate to many of the questions and concerns that people have during the process. In this chapter, I'll try to help you make sense of all the legalese and give you the confidence you need to set out on this new journey all by yourself.

Divorce is fundamentally about ending a marriage in law. Although the emotional toll and the legal ramifications are inextricably intertwined, it is essential to keep them separate. If you are considering divorce, it is in your best interest to familiarize yourself with the applicable laws so that you may make educated decisions and chart a course that is in line with your goals.

Knowing the exact rules and regulations regulating divorce in your jurisdiction will set you up for success as you begin this path. It's important to do your homework and learn the specific laws that apply to your circumstance because they can differ widely depending on where you live.

Divorce has a bad rap because of the widespread notion that it's a zero-sum game in which one spouse always loses and the other always wins. But rather than approaching the process with the mindset of an adversarial conflict, it is vital to shift gears and go in with the aim of pursuing equitable answers. The end result should be an equitable distribution of property, obligations, and duties that takes into account your individual position.

An expert family law attorney should be consulted for advice throughout the divorce procedure. An attorney can act as your representative in court, giving you guidance and representation while you deal with the legal system. They will make sure you know what you may expect and what you can do. With their help, you may feel at ease knowing that your best interests are being represented throughout any negotiations, mediation, or court processes.

Divorce is a complex legal procedure, and as you learn more, you'll find that many different types of legal paperwork play important roles. At first appearance, legal documents including petitions, replies, and agreements can be intimidating. Read each paper carefully and consult your lawyer if you have any questions. You will be in a better position to make educated decisions and actively participate in the process if you take the time to familiarize yourself with the contents of these documents and fully grasp their relevance.

Child custody and support agreements are other essential factors to think about when a family includes children. Your primary concern should be for your kids' safety at all times. Learn the rules and regulations regarding child support and custody in your area. Try to work out a parenting arrangement that benefits your kids both emotionally and financially. Try to build a co-parenting plan with your ex that allows for continuity and stability in your children's lives by working together whenever possible.

Recognizing the mental and emotional strain that divorce can cause is crucial. Taking care of yourself has utmost importance during this time of change. If you feel you need help navigating the emotional issues that may develop, reach out to friends, family, therapists, or support groups. Keep in mind that you have people rooting for you and that asking for help is a sign of strength, not weakness, on this path.

It is important to keep in mind that the rules and processes governing divorce are put in place to protect the interests of both parties.

Trust the legal system and the professionals who can help you through it, even if it seems daunting at times. Your lawyer is there to advise you and look out for your best interests throughout the process.

By learning as much as you can about the divorce law system, you are actively participating in the creation of your future, my dear reader. Take advantage of this chance to improve your perspective, knowledge, and agency. The legalities may seem overwhelming but know that you have support. Seek out legal and emotional aid as you work through the process. Have faith in your ability to bounce back from setbacks and know that you can accomplish anything you set your mind to.

Chapter Five

Co-Parenting: Prioritizing Children's Well-being

Co-parenting has been one of the most difficult and gratifying aspects of my own divorce experience. My ex-spouse and I have three lovely children who are the centers of our lives, and we had to figure out how to navigate this new terrain while making their well-being our top priority. In this chapter, I will discuss some of the lessons I've learned about co-parenting so far in the hopes that they will be helpful to you as you continue on this journey along with your co-parent.

Co-parenting is a long-term relationship that calls for honest and open dialogue, mutual respect, and a dedication to putting the children's needs first at all times. It's not easy, but with hard work and a common goal, it can lead to a more peaceful and supportive home life for your kids.

Many people believe that if they want to successfully co-parent, they must become best friends with their former partner. Establishing a respectful and cooperative dynamic centered on the needs of the children is more vital than maintaining cordial ties. Maintain an open line of communication about parenting time and other arrangements, as well as decisions and concerns, while yet giving each parent space to pursue their interests.

Co-parenting works best when both parents are committed to maintaining a consistent routine. Creating stability and predictability for your children requires establishing clear guidelines for custody arrangements, visitation schedules, and shared obligations. Find a middle ground that allows children to flourish in both homes and takes into account their emotional needs, academic obligations, and extracurricular interests.

In order to co-parent successfully, open lines of communication are essential. Find a way to communicate with your ex that both of you are comfortable with, whether that's in person, over the phone, or through the mail. The needs of the kids should be your top priority at all times. If you want to keep your co-parenting relationship strong, you should avoid arguments and sensitive topics that could cause friction. Instead, keep things professional by focusing on the youngster and talking to them in a way that shows respect.

As a co-parent, adaptability is a skill you must develop. Due to the unpredictability of life, it is often necessary to make changes to previously stated plans. It's possible to build collaboration and understanding between parents by adopting a flexible mindset and showing a willingness to adapt to new circumstances. Keep in mind that no matter what happens, your primary responsibility is to be a rock for your kids.

It's crucial to keep your kids out of the middle of whatever drama you and your ex could be having. Your kids should grow up in an atmosphere of love and safety, unburdened by your arguments. When talking about the other parent, watch your vocabulary to make sure it's respectful and upbeat. Foster honest and open lines of communication with your kids, and let them vent their emotions without fear of reprisal.

Finally, ask for help if you feel you need it. Having a strong support system is crucial when going through the emotional ups and downs of co-parenting. Get involved in a support group or hang out with someone you know who has experience co-parenting. Having the opportunity to learn from and find solace in the words and actions of those who have been where you are now is a priceless resource.

As a parent who has been through a divorce and knows the challenges you will face, I am here to support you as a co-parent. Keep in mind that there is always something new to learn about co-parenting. Keep your cool as you, your ex, and the kids figure out the ins and outs of joint parenting.

A caring and secure foundation can be established for your children by prioritizing their well-being, encouraging open communication, and creating a supportive environment.

Chapter Six

Self-Care and Healing:

Rediscovering Your Identity

Divorce brings about a lot of emotional upheavals, and in the midst of that, it can be easy to lose sight of who you are. The breakdown of a marriage can make one feel as if they have lost their sense of self. This trying adventure, however, can be used as a springboard for personal development and discovery. This section is all about you taking care of yourself and being well so that you may get back in touch with who you are and embark on exciting new adventures.

It is more important than ever to put yourself first when life seems chaotic and uncertain. It's not a nice-to-have; it's a must-have. When you practice self-care, you make a conscious effort to look after your own emotional, mental, and physiological well. Keep in mind that you are deserving of rest and relaxation despite the chaos and activity around you.

Each person's path to recovery requires a customized strategy; there is no universal panacea. As you begin this process of metamorphosis, though, you have options. Let's look at a few different forms of self-care that might help you feel better and get through this time in your life.

1. Care for one's own emotions: Divorce can cause a roller coaster of feelings, from sadness and fury to

bewilderment and relief. Allow yourself to experience and work through these feelings. Seek help from a trained expert in the form of therapy or counseling.

Do things that make you feel better, such as writing in a notebook, practicing meditation, or connecting with others in a similar situation. Give yourself permission to feel and acknowledge your feelings without fear of criticism.

2. Physical self-care: Taking care of yourself physically can be a potent tool in reestablishing your sense of self. Take some form of exercise every day, even if it's only a stroll outside. Nourish your body with meals that will help it function at its best, and make eating healthfully a top priority. Get plenty of shut-eye, as this can help restore your

energy and clear your head. Yoga and tai chi are two holistic disciplines that can help you heal on all levels, physically and mentally.

3. Take care of yourself socially by establishing a group of friends and family who will always have your back. If you need someone to talk to, someone to lean on, or someone to hug you can find that person within your friends and family. Engage in fun gatherings where you can meet others who share your interests. Keep in mind that you are not alone on this path and that there are people who understand and can offer support because they have been there.

4. Self-care that focuses on the mind and intellectual pursuits is a powerful tool for regaining

motivation and clarity. Learn more about subjects that are important to your development by reading books that inspire and motivate you. Take advantage of the opportunity to learn something new and broaden your horizons by signing up for a workshop or course that interests you. Develop interests that stimulate your imagination, both as a means of satisfying your need to express yourself and as a welcome diversion from whatever difficulties you may be experiencing.

5. Self-care that focuses on your spiritual health can be a source of comfort and calm in the midst of turmoil. Try out different methods until you find one that works for you, whether it's praying, meditating, or going outside. Think about what you hold dear and why, and try to find some common

ground with your inner self. You could find that the advice of spiritual leaders or the study of ideologies that resonate with your own journey is helpful.

Take care of yourself; doing so is an act of love and preservation for yourself, not of being selfish. Taking time for oneself is crucial, no matter how hectic or turbulent your life may appear. Accept that recovery will take some time and try to enjoy the ride. Take it easy on yourself and give yourself the chance to change and develop in ways that are meaningful to you.

It's crucial to treat yourself with kindness and compassion as you embark on this self-care and healing journey. Keep in mind that recovery is not a one-step procedure. There will be days when you feel strong and capable of taking on the world, and there will be days when you feel weak and exposed. Accept the ups and downs of your feelings and give yourself permission to feel them fully.

Creating limits for yourself is an important part of self-care. It's natural to feel torn in several directions throughout a divorce, whether it's dealing with the legal process, co-parenting, or settling into a new home. In the face of so many pressures, it's essential to set limits that safeguard your health and happiness. Master the art of the firm "no" when necessary, and put happiness-inducing pursuits first. Keep in mind that you need time and space to concentrate on your recovery process.

Taking care of yourself isn't just about rewarding yourself with short-term pleasures; it's also about establishing long-term routines that support your health and happiness.

Include self-care activities in your daily schedule, even if just in baby steps. Try to seek out times of quiet reflection and meditation. Pursue what makes you happy, be it a specific interest, time spent in nature, or just a quiet moment with a cup of tea.

It's human nature to want to get better quickly, but healing is a process that can't be rushed. Learn to ride out the ups and downs with patience and kindness toward yourself. Give yourself permission to feel sad about the loss, but also to rejoice in your own resiliency. No matter how tiny, progress is always worth celebrating.

Keep in mind that you have support while you work through this phase of recovery and self-care. Get help from someone you trust, such as friends, family, or professionals. Create a support system of people who will cheer you on when the going gets tough. Keep in mind that your path to redefining who you are after a divorce will be different from anyone else's.

Keep an open mind about what can happen next on your new journey. Take this time to focus on who you really are, what you're truly passionate about, and how you can make your life reflect that. Healing is a chance to reimagine what happened, accept the lessons it taught you, and go forward with newfound strength and insight.

Chapter Seven

Financial Adjustment: Creating a New Plan

One of the most difficult aspects of readjusting to single life following a divorce is the financial one. As you set out on this new path, take on the task of establishing a solid financial foundation upon which to construct a secure future for yourself.

You may re-create your future of financial freedom and stability like a competent artist with a clean slate. This unfamiliar environment may appear intimidating at first, but with focus and confidence, you can succeed.

Taking stock of where you are financially is the initial stroke in this painting. Look at your possessions, debts, and income sources with compassion and candor. Having a firm grasp on your financial situation will serve as a rock around which to build the choices you make in the future. It is essential to compile all pertinent data, including financial records, investment holdings, and existing obligations. Consider it the methodical process of revealing the true shape of your financial tapestry.

After getting a firm grasp on your current financial situation, it's time to start planning for the future. Tell me about your near- and far-term objectives. Want to buy a house, open a business, or send your kids to college? Let your hopes and aspirations inspire you to take action. You can start planning your route to success by picturing your final destination in detail.

Let's start painting using the financial tools at our disposal. Here's where you can use some colorful language. Visualize yourself as an artist, using your financial skills to create a masterpiece of security and fortitude.

The budgeting process is a crucial skill because it gives life to your financial goals. Create a budget with forethought, making sure to set aside money for savings and personal development in addition to paying the bills. Think about using an app or other digital tool that can keep track of your expenditures and hold you accountable. With each deliberate purchase, you'll have a better idea of where your money is going and how it may best support your new priorities.

Diversification, a kaleidoscope of bright hues that adds strength and safety to your financial painting, is another brushstroke to think about. You should diversify your portfolio by investing in several types of assets, such as stocks, bonds, and real estate. The volatile stock market can be weathered with the help of diversification, which can also open up new avenues for growth.

Don't forget to include the power of education in your financial masterpiece. Get lost in a rainbow of economic knowledge and agency. Learn as much as you can about managing your money, making investments, and saving for retirement. Growing one's store of information gives one the assurance to act decisively and change with the times.

Working together is a priceless addition to the painting. Consult a qualified financial expert, such as a certified public accountant or a certified financial planner, for assistance. They can be reliable allies on your path to financial security and autonomy, offering advice and assistance along the way.

In conclusion, keep in mind that financial readjustment is a process, a lovely evolution of development and change. Your own financial strategy will undergo gradual adjustments, much like an artist's method. Accept the brushstrokes of trial and error, and give yourself permission to make changes as you go. Take your time and be gentle with yourself as you explore this unfamiliar territory; every decision you make now will affect the final product.

Chapter Eight

Embracing the Future: Setting Goals and New Beginnings

Now that one act of your life has come to an end, you may begin the next with all the promise and promise of a fresh start. In this section, we'll construct a vivid picture of our hopes and dreams for the future by making plans and looking forward to them.

Picture yourself as the hero of your own novel, about to enter a world of limitless possibility. Creating the future you want is the opening act of this enormous drama. Which hopes do you cherish the most? What hidden interests have been quietly waiting for you? Give yourself permission to delve deeply into your dreams. Don't be afraid to follow the imaginative language used in your dreams.

Let's take the future into our own hands and start painting it with the help of goal-setting. The vivid brushstrokes that give form and function to your dreams are your goals. It's best to get started with manageable objectives that will both satisfy your immediate needs and help you gain momentum. Achieving these intermediate objectives can be thought of as building blocks on the road to your ultimate purpose.

Be understanding and empathetic to yourself as you continue to put your hopes and goals onto paper for the future. On this path of self-discovery, treat yourself with kindness and compassion. Recognize your inner fortitude and tenacity by honoring even the smallest of victories.

Visualization is a strong tool that can help you along your journey. Visualize the life you want to be living, then close your eyes.

Just try to conjure up the sight and smell and sound of this place. Imagine yourself achieving all of your aspirations and dreams. Use these pictures to inspire you and direct your efforts.

Goal-setting is essential, but so is the willingness to start over. You can create a brand new beginning just like a playwright creates an engaging prologue. Embrace the imaginative vocabulary of your fresh starts, and don't be afraid to try something new. Think about starting again by doing something different with your life, whether that's changing careers, going back to school, or volunteering. Take advantage of your independence to reinvent yourself and build a life that truly speaks to you.

Keep in mind that there may likely be obstacles to overcome. Life is full of surprises, just like a good novel. Take advantage of the situation by viewing the difficulties as learning experiences. You should change your direction and your objectives if necessary, but you should never lose sight of the big picture.

Put yourself in the company of positive and encouraging people as you embark on your new journey. Find other people who can motivate and encourage you. Talk to people you trust about your goals and aspirations, and get involved in groups that share your passions. By banding together, you may establish a safety net of encouragement and friendship that will carry you through.

And finally, let appreciation be the beacon that leads the way. Gratitude for past experiences, inner fortitude, and future possibilities should be voiced. Gratitude is the stroke that paints your journey with happiness and pleasure, prompting you to savor the now even as you strive for the future.

Keep in mind that you write your own ending as you look forward to the future and plan for fresh starts. Paint a vivid picture of your hopes and ambitions using inventive language. Visualize your ideal future, accept the possibility of change, and commit to achieving your goals. Be understanding and kind to yourself; enjoy your progress.

Put yourself in a positive environment with encouraging people and learn to appreciate right now. You are painting a beautiful picture of a life well-lived with every stroke of your brush.

Chapter Nine

Rebuilding Relationships: Family and Friends

Divorce has the potential to put a strain on any existing connections. But within the area of reconstruction comes the chance to give new life to connections that are essential to you, connections with family and friends that can become even stronger and more robust. In this chapter, we begin the process of mending these treasured bonds through the use of inventive diction.

Think of your bonds with others as delicate tapestries, weaved together with the strands of your love, trust, and shared experiences. Some of those links may have become frayed because of the divorce, but they are not broken. You may repair and strengthen these ties, weaving a web of love and friendship in the process.

Recognizing the effects of divorce on all parties is the first step toward mending relationships. You and your ex-spouse aren't the only ones who will feel the impact. Those close to you may have had a similar sense of loss and turmoil. Show empathy and common ground by listening attentively and providing a secure environment for honest communication. Be open and honest with your personal feelings to help them empathize with your experience and give them a chance to do the same.

Keep in mind the healing salve of forgiveness as you make your way through this difficult process.

To forgive is not to ignore or minimize hurt felt, but rather to make a conscious decision to let go of resentment and bitterness. When you forgive, you set yourself free and make room for healing and development. Accept forgiveness as a transformative tool and watch as it restores broken bonds.

Rebuilding bridges between people also requires the creative use of language. Use kind, compassionate, and accepting language when interacting with those you care about. Express your sincere need for reconciliation and reconnection in your choice of words. Express your genuine affection, thanks, and desire to mend ties with those you care about.

Actions, together with words, are the strokes that paint the picture of your intentions. Make an appearance for your loved ones to show that you are serious about mending the bridges to your most important relationships. Make an effort to keep in touch with these people on a regular basis, whether it's through phone conversations, in-person get-togethers, or mutual interests. Your actions should speak loudly about your sincerity and commitment to mending fences and forging new bonds.

Relationship repair requires effort on both sides. Keep your arms and heart wide open. Don't be afraid to put yourself out there by telling your loved ones what you want and need. Pay close attention as they talk, confirming their experiences and building trust by showing you understand their point of view. Your relationship with yourself is also an important one to repair. Recognize the importance of prioritizing your own health and adopting a self-compassionate, self-care stance. Focus on what makes you happy and fulfilled, and use that time for introspection and development. Reconstructing your sense of self enables you to better support the development and success of your relationships.

Finally, approach this process of reconnecting with others with patience and persistence. Similar to how tending to a landscape can take time and effort, so can tending to a relationship. Know that there will be ups and downs and that you must be resilient in the face of any obstacles. Take it all in stride, and let the imaginative lexicon of affection, comprehension, and development lead the way.

Chapter Ten

Conclusion: Embracing the Journey Ahead

Let us pause at this journey's end to consider the discoveries we've made about ourselves and the healing and progress we've experienced as a group. When things seemed hopeless, the book "Divorce: A New Adventure" was there to provide comfort, direction, and light. Let's end this chapter by looking forward to the next one with loving, encouraging words of encouragement.

Divorce is not a path anyone wants to take, but it is one that can be traveled with dignity and fortitude.

The depths of our emotions, the difficulties we face, and the transformational potential of self-care, financial adjustment, goal-setting, and repairing relationships have all been discussed in these pages. We have recognized our own power and learned that fresh starts are possible even in the middle of chaos.

You've arrived at a new beginning, and I hope you'll welcome it with open arms and a loving heart. Self-love is the most important thing you can give yourself at this point. Respect for those bonds that have lasted the test of time and enthusiasm for those that have yet to be created.

Keep in mind that love is the bedrock upon which we construct our lives as you continue on this journey. A deep appreciation for the beauty and simplicity of the here and now. Love for the future and all its potential, for the hopes and dreams that have been reawakened in you.

Let love be your compass as you navigate difficulties. If you truly care about yourself, you'll give yourself the compassion and care you need to heal and flourish.

Show your love for others around you by being patient, compassionate, and forgiving. Accept the wonders and wonderment of the world with love.

Take the next step with gusto and enthusiasm. Consider the curves in the road ahead as chances to learn and develop. Permit yourself to have an adventurous mindset, openness to new experiences, and willingness to move beyond your comfort zone.

Always keep in mind that you have support, even in your darkest moments of uncertainty. The stories told here have brought us together as a group and fostered mutual respect and compassion. Get in touch with people who care about you, people who have been where you are, and experts who can help you out. If we stick together, we can get through anything and share in each victory.

As we wrap up this book, I want to reassure you that this is not the end of your adventure. This is a continual journey with many turns, successes, and difficulties. Know that you are powerful, capable, and worthy of a life that is rich with happiness and meaning, and live each day to the fullest.

Your path forward, may it be illuminated by the imaginative vocabulary of love and encouragement. Take on the road ahead with a soul that can't be broken, a head that can't be beaten, and a heart that can't be contained. The future is blank, waiting to be filled in by your bravery, grace, and undying faith in the potential of fresh starts.

With deep appreciation and affection, I say goodbye to this part of our journey together. Your future be rosy, your heart joyful, and your soul unbreakable. Take the next step forward and build a life that is truly yours, one that is rich with love, joy, and infinite potential.

www.ingramcontent.com/pod-product-compliance
Lightning Source LLC
Chambersburg PA
CBHW070848220526
45466CB00005B/1929